How to Make Sh*t Happen

Make more money, get in better shape, create epic relationships and control your life!

By Sean Whalen
Founder of LIONS NOT SHEEP

How to Make Sh*t Happen
Make more money, get in better shape, create epic relationships
and control your life!

ISBN: 9781984268945

Imprint: Independently published

Cover design by Jason Woodrich

Edited by Kathryn Tague-DeHoyos

This book is dedicated to my mom.
The most faithful, selfless, inspired and loving woman I know.
You are my hero, Momma.

Foreword

Introduction

The Single Greatest Lesson

POWER

The Body

PASSION

Relationships

PURPOSE

The Mind & Spirit

PRODUCTION

Business

Conclusion

**"True potential is treasure.
Core 4 is the map."**

- Cory Cooley

Foreword

***

Life ain't easy. Nothing about it is. Whoever tells you to just "hope," or to "think positive thoughts," and things will work out, I can guarantee hasn't accomplished shit.

Around every corner, we see and hear a thousand "successful" people selling every way to "get rich quick," or, "fix your problems overnight," but where do we hear, "Get rich FOR SURE," or, "fix your problems FOR SURE?" Nowhere, except from a select few. Why? Because selling hard ass work for a long ass time is not as profitable a venture as selling fast cash & overnight success.

Life takes work. Business takes work. Marriage takes work. Being in shape takes work. And most days it takes a fucking TON of work.

HARD WORK!

***

When Sean and I met on social media I knew he believed & understood this. I saw him with his kids, I saw him with his business and clients, I knew this guy got it the way I got it.

After meeting him, hanging out with him, shooting guns with him and having our share of whiskeys together, I knew Sean not only believed what he preached, but he fucking lived it.

In a world of talkers, Sean is a doer. In a world of sensitive flowers who want things handed to them, Sean is stepping up and doing the work.

This book is simple. The message is simple. That's why I like it. There is no bullshit here. If you do the things in this book you will make shit happen. I'm not saying you will make millions overnight, but this book is a recipe for success in any area of life.

It will take A LOT of work on your part.

Daily commitment to daily action.

Rituals and work every single day.

How is that a bad thing? That's the fun part. The part you'll look back on in 20 years and proud of!

I went from sleeping on a piss stained mattress in the back of my first supplement store to driving Lamborghinis and doing whatever the fuck I want...when I want...with who I want.

I did it by working my ass off and building habits of success.

I did it by doing exactly what Sean talks about in this book.

Working hard but working SMART.

Doing simple shit every day, not trying to hit a home run every time.

I did it by creating a plan, writing that shit down, being a good person, asking lots of questions, learning from my mistakes, surrounding myself with great people, exiting relationships that no longer aligned with me, taking care of my body and my relationships, and working my fucking ass off.

Do the shit in this book.

Not tomorrow, not next week, not when your dog tells you to, or when shit gets easier or you when you have more time because that'll never happen.

What you do TODAY...

What you eat TODAY...

How you train TODAY...

The investments you make in yourself TODAY...

...will all shape the person you are tomorrow, next week, next year & for the rest of your life.

Use this tool.

Or don't.

The world needs fry cooks too.

-Andy Frisella
1st Phorm Founder and CEO

Introduction

***

I was juggling bowling balls.

I remember not too long before I burned my entire business, marriage, and life to the ground feeling like I was juggling bowling balls. Feeling like I was doing everything I could just to keep my head above water, to keep the wife and kids happy, and to keep my 170+ employees excited and motivated to keep making millions.

I remember waking up day after day looking in the mirror saying, "ok mother fucker, make today your bitch!"

Sure, I listened to all the rah rah rah stuff online. I listened to the motivational talks; I bought planners and cool apps to keep me organized. I had personal assistants, a personnel admin for my business, managers, managers for the managers, but every day was CHAOS.

I felt like I was working 100 hours a day but never really getting ahead. Yeah, we were making a ton of money, and on the surface, everything was kosher, but behind the scenes, there were some serious problems.

I had some serious fucking problems.

I had built this life, business, and family. But it was absolute CHAOS.

Imagine putting your head in the blender and turning it on. It was kinda like that.

I had all the shit you were supposed to have as a successful entrepreneur, but as the saying goes, I was burning the candle at both ends.

I'd take the family to Disneyland, but I'd be on my blackberry (old school I know) the entire time.

I'd be at the office and put in a 20-hour day but would still feel like I was not getting ahead and needed to be home or with the kids.

I had houses, vacation houses, vacations, a ski boat, cars and all the other crap that costs tens of thousands of dollars each month.

CHAOS.

That is the best way for me to describe my life back then.

It was easy to bullshit everyone around you with four cars and a Rolex, but my life was fucking CHAOS.

I had all these people in my life that I was "working for" and providing for, but at the end of it all, something was very wrong.

I'd show up at the office and would bounce from thing to thing, meeting to meeting, and have a dozen of my employees come in yapping with me, all before lunch.

Some of this stuff was planned.

Most of it was not.

My wife knew I was not a "home for dinner at 5pm guy" because I was a business owner. I was an entrepreneur. What we were doing back then was hustling 20 hours a day for a few years to set up the rest of our lives. Work hard now so we can have all the fun and enjoy all the money later.

Retiring at 30 was the goal.

$150,000 a month of passive income was the goal.

We were on our way when one day it happened.

CHAOS won.

I fucking lost it.

I was losing millions in bankruptcy because the real estate market crash of 2008 kicked my ass.

But at the same time, I was making tons of money flipping tax deeds and foreclosed homes. The REO market was on FIRE, and I was crushing it!

I was in the office hustling; I was traveling the country growing the business; I was home when I could be home. And I was eating lunch only if I was taking a client.

Oh, and in between all that cool shit I was dealing with attorneys and creditors during a very humiliating, multimillion-dollar bankruptcy.

All of this finally took its toll.

I quit juggling the bowling balls, and I walked away from it all.

No more business.

No more family.

No more magazine covers.

One day I met my business partner for breakfast, and I handed him a single sheet of paper. On that paper, it simply stated I was turning all my interest in this multimillion-dollar company over to him and taking nothing in return. I walked away with nothing.

My wife and I divorced. I shut her down emotionally.

I got rid of all the shit, left the 8,500-square-foot house, and turned my entire world off.

Mid-life crisis.

Mental break down.

Call it whatever the fuck you want, I simply quit playing the game.

I quit juggling the bowling balls.

I shut down emotionally, spiritually, and physically, and walked away from it all.

The weight of everything took its toll.

The life of "success" I had built, the success I had—by the world's standards—became too fucking heavy, and juggling everything, and everyone and all the blah blah blah came to an end.

I had officially burned out.

***

A lot of people went through the same shit in 2008.

Lots of my buddies and business partners lost it all. Many of them ended up divorced and broke. Many of them, to this day, years and years later, still blame that time for why their life is shit.

I had my own personal pity party. I buried my head in the sand (more like stuck it up my ass). I was VERY angry.

I blamed everyone.

I hated and blamed my ex-wife for not supporting me.

I blamed my business partner for not helping more.

I blamed my friends for walking away from me when shit got hard.

I was ANGRY.

So angry that one night after drinking, spewing my bullshit, trying to call my ex-wife only to be hung up on (not surprised), I put my 9mm in my mouth.

I laid on my bed with tears streaming down my face trying to rationalize with myself how it would be better for my three young kids to grow up without their wrecking ball of a father.

I had an angel on one shoulder saying how I couldn't do it because I was a good guy and just going through a rough spot.

I had a different angel on the other shoulder telling me I was a piece of shit who had ruined all my employees lives; destroyed a perfectly good marriage, and I was never going to amount to anything other than a pile of useless shit because I'd lost millions and burned so many bridges.

I'll never forget the taste of gunpowder and oil.

I pray you never experience this. I pray you never taste that taste.

After a night that took me down the deepest most terrifying and painful rabbit hole of darkness, I woke up the next morning with the pistol a few inches from my head, a bottle of whiskey on the nightstand, and a pit in my stomach.

I knew I could not keep going in this direction.

I was fucking killing myself.

I knew that me banging my head against the wall over and over with all this anger was simply insane, and never going to get me good results. I knew bullshitting and lying about how I "was good" every time people asked was not sustainable. I knew that the pain and frustration were not going to help me accomplish anything. I knew if I kept going this way one night that gun was going to go off.

So, I did the hardest thing I had ever done. I did the thing that an "alpha male," such as myself, never does. I did the thing I had NEVER done before.

I reached out for help.

***

One of my friends, who had gone through a similar situation as mine, had hired a coach and I watched him start to change. He went through a weekend-long men's program with a few other guys, where they did a bunch of physical shit and at the same time started opening up about their fears and lies etc. All the soft "girly" shit real men never do (or so I thought).

I noticed him changing.

He had lost a lot of money and ended up divorcing as well, but as I watched him over a month or so, I saw him start to change.

So, I went to his office one day and asked him what he was doing.

"I'm reading books and meditating in the morning," he said.

"Come on bro, meditating? That's hippy bullshit, what are you really doing."

"I'm serious," he said, "I'm putting myself first, organizing my time, and taking control of my life."

To make a long story short, I bought in.

What was the worst that could happen? I'd learn to meditate and read some new books, that couldn't be bad I thought. Shit, nothing I was doing had been working!

So, I went all in, and I attended the same weekend retreat he did.

It was a group of other fuck up's, much like me. Guys who burned their lives to the ground, guys struggling with insecurity, guilt, shame, etc.

Guys who said, "I'm good" when inside they were SCREAMING out for help.

It's funny how we all think we are islands. I believed no one could possibly know how bad I hurt, how bad the divorce was, how hard it was to make money or be present for my kids.

The experience taught me principles I had never heard before, principles that had been passed down through generations and written about in books like, *The War of Art*, and *The Way of the Superior Man*.

Participating in the retreat with these men, hiring a coach, and finally acknowledging that I did not know it all, lead me on a journey of self-discovery that has RADICALLY changed my life for the better.

I think the biggest step for me was saying something that has helped me create a lot of success:

I KNOW WHAT I DON'T KNOW.

I knew what I knew but I finally admitted that I knew there was SO MUCH I did NOT know.

So, I began practicing all this stuff I learned.

I began meditating.

I structured my day. I had a plan for my day that worked with no CHAOS!

I'd never experienced this before!

The ability to control my mind, my time, my schedule, and most of all my LIFE.

It was SO radically different than anything I had ever experienced, but there is something that I could not deny about all of it. IT WORKED.

I was getting RESULTS.

My mind was getting clearer, I started making more money, my relationships were becoming real, and I felt good!

:-)

So that, my friends, is why I have decided to write this book.

Over the last three years, I have had Facebook videos and posts liked, shared, and commented on over 500,000,000 times.

One night I shared a Facebook post in 2015, and I did something I had not done before on social media. I TOLD THE TRUTH. And that post went viral.

Tens of millions of likes and shares just on that one post. It launched me into the public eye, and I discovered that the more I told my story—and the TRUTH behind me—the more this tribe of people grew.

Since then, I have launched multiple businesses, including a global coaching and consulting company called LIONS NOT SHEEP, where I help people and businesses do one specific thing.

GET HUGE RESULTS.

***

I have coached thousands of people.

I've spoken in front of thousands of people.

I've shared the stage with the likes of Gary Vaynerchuk.

And most importantly, I've had the opportunity to help thousands of men and women strengthen their marriages, make more money, get in better shape, and create the life they want.

Yeah, the guy who put a gun in his mouth because he couldn't figure out how to get control was now teaching people how to control their lives!

So why listen to what I have to say here in this book? Why listen to anything I have to say at all?

Because I fucking did it.

I don't have every answer. What I do have is REAL LIFE experience with suicide, depression, business, bankruptcy, making millions, losing millions, building a business from scratch, divorce, lawyers and courts, rebuilding with my ex, being a father, owning multiple companies while being a good dad, and whole bunch of other fun and crazy shit!

I have done all this coaching and teaching around one single principle I learned from my coaches, and which I have practiced and mastered through my own personal journey.

A tool which has helped me accomplish not only all that cool stuff I just mentioned but has helped me build an amazing relationship and friendship with my ex-wife.

A tool that has helped me become a better, more connected father. And most of all has helped me build a life where I am in control.

I control my day.

I control my finances.

I control my body and fitness.

I learned how to get exactly what I want in all the areas of my life.

***

In the following chapters, I'm going to share with you the single greatest lesson I have ever learned and developed.

The one thing I now do that has saved my life, made me more money, helped get me into the best shape of my life, and made me capable of building lasting and powerful relationships.

I am on a journey just like you, and I believe in teaching from experience, NOT theory.

There is NO THEORY in this book.

I only share exact and specific lessons I have learned from exact and specific actions I have taken.

If I have not done it, I don't tell you to try it.

***

From the gun in my mouth to speaking in front of thousands.

From CHAOS and bankruptcy to helping CEOs and business owners make more money while working less.

This has been my journey, and this is the single greatest lesson I have ever learned.

- Sean

"Core 4—when applied—is the guide to living a productive and successful life. It has helped me have clarity and not chaos. Core 4 means a better quality of life for myself and my family. Core 4 is the best gift you can give to yourself. Every day you will have accomplished the most important things in life by doing these 4 simple yet amazing steps."

- Jose Galvan

The Single Greatest Lesson

✳✳✳

I was asked once, "if you could only share one message, or teach one thing for the rest of your life, what would it be?"

It's a simple answer.

CORE 4.

I would teach people exactly what it is, how it works, and why it is the single greatest thing I have ever learned, studied, and practiced.

CORE 4 saved my life.

CORE 4 is the exact tool I used to go from the bottom of the barrel to building a multi-million-dollar global brand. It is the tool that took me from having a gun in my mouth to smiling non-stop.

CHAOS is the enemy of good fitness, a profitable business, deep and connected relationships, and a clear mind. CHAOS produces shitty results.

CORE 4 is CLARITY.

CORE 4 is POWER.

CORE 4 is literally the source and foundation of everything for me.

Every single day, every action you and I take, every experience you and I have, falls into one of 4 categories.

Everything we do and experience involves our body, our relationships, our mind, and by extension our business.

It is all directly connected to CORE 4.

EVERYTHING.

There is nothing that happens in my day that does not fit into CORE 4.

There is nothing I could create that fits outside of CORE 4.

***

SO, WHAT THE HELL IS CORE 4?

CORE 4 is simply this:

- POWER - (body)
- PASSION - (relationships)
- PURPOSE - (the mind)
- PRODUCTION - (business)

When we talk about CORE 4, we are talking about each of these areas in their entirety.

Everything happening each day comes from – or is related to – one (or all) of these things.

- Your BODY.
- Your RELATIONSHIPS.
- Your MIND.

- Your BUSINESS.

Your literal and physical BODY.

Your RELATIONSHIPS, not only intimate but family, friends, co-workers, children, etc.

Your MIND, and the ability you have to fill it with positive thoughts and valuable and useful knowledge.

Your BUSINESS, income, and financial security.

Everything that happens, every day, falls into one of these four areas.

Everything you want to create or do fits within one of these four areas.

Every goal you will ever set, inside CORE 4.

Every dream you ever have, inside CORE 4.

Everything from the kid's soccer game to having sex applies to CORE 4.

Every aspect of your life IS CORE 4.

***

What would it look like if you could wake up knowing you only had four things to do each day to create big results?

What would it look like if you went from having a massive to-do list on a project, to being able to narrow it down to small, attainable actions every day, to get to the big result?

What would life look like if you could manage the WORK/HOME balance with ease and simplicity vs. always feeling like you are failing at one or the other?

What would life look like if you had NO DRAMA with anyone else?

What would life look like if you could hit the gym and feed your mind every morning without feeling rushed or like you should be at the office already?

***

This is CORE 4.

It's how you eat the elephant.

You can try to fit the entire elephant in your mouth, but it's obvious that won't work. The insanity of life though, is that we will try and try and try to eat the entire thing in one bite.

The elephants are our goals.

Better relationships, big goals at work and the office, building a better body. These are the elephants.

It's physically impossible, and no matter how cool you think you are, to fit the entire elephant in your mouth at one time.

So, how DO you eat the elephant? (get fit, get the work projects done, build relationships, sharpen your mind, etc.)

ONE BITE AT A TIME.

SMALL BITES EVERY SINGLE DAY. Tiny small bites over and over.

CORE 4 is your knife and fork to eat every elephant in your life.

***

CORE 4 is NOT NEGOTIABLE.

I repeat, CORE 4 IS NOT FUCKING NEGOTIABLE.

24/7. 365.

Every single day you invest in all four areas.

Every single day you do VERY SPECIFIC and VERY INTENTIONAL actions in each area of your life, each area of CORE 4.

When I was in the midst of the CHAOS, everything seemed to run together. Nothing was clear and concise. When there was an issue with one thing, there always seemed to be issues with other things as well.

I tell people, "HOW YOU DO ONE THING IS HOW YOU DO EVERYTHING." Because, for the most part, if a person is lying in their business, they are lying in other areas of their life, as well.

If a person is slacking in their workouts and fitness, they are typically slacking at date night with their lover and have rarely found consistency in reading/studying. If they are stressed all day at the office, they typically bring that stress and bullshit home with them.

CORE 4 is the SIMPLE and CLEAR system I use to break down every action, every day.

It is the tool you need to move forward in each of the four areas with INTENTION and PURPOSE.

Every single day.

***

Here is an example:

Having a work/life balance is a struggle for many.

As a business owner/entrepreneur, this was a struggle for me, too. I was always working.

When I was at the office, I was working. When I was home, I was answering messages, emails, calls... I was always on, always working. It was my company and my job, so it's what I "had" to do.

I explained to my wife that this is how it was if we wanted to make lots of cash, retire early, and live all of our dreams.

I would be with the kids, but I was not truly present with them because I was texting or emailing. Facebook wasn't even a thing at this point. Now that we have social media, smartphones, and all that shit to add into this mix, no wonder most business owners/ entrepreneurs are distracted and completely fucked! I was distracted and not present, and all I had was a non-smart, non-touchscreen, old-school fucking blackberry!

What happened to me is happening to MILLIONS of people right now.

My wife would get mad because I was always on my phone working, even when we were at the beach or in line at Disney. Her being mad would piss me off because me being on my phone was what was "providing" for us to be doing all this stuff.

In the mix of all this, I'd get mad and pissed off because she was "acting ungrateful," but she would be pissed because I was never present.

My kids experienced only a fraction of my attention because I was mad at mom, working, and trying to juggle it all.

It was a vicious cycle, and no one was ever happy.

It was CHAOS.

CHAOS inside me, which created CHAOS outside me.

She was mad, and that made me mad. I was mad, and that made her mad.

It was a vicious cycle, and I see millions of people stuck in this cycle.

To this day, it all still seems like a blur, and I never really found a way to get CLEAR on anything.

It was like I was hunting deer with a shotgun. Shooting and shooting. But, I could never hit anything. It was only when I realized that CORE 4 was my rifle for hunting that I finally figured out how to get the results I wanted, and actually hit the deer!

Instead of just shooting and shooting hoping I would hit something, I learned how to take aim and with one shot hit my target.

CORE 4 was the tool that let me become specific and intentional with my thoughts and actions.

CORE 4 is the tool I use every single day of my life to get exactly what I want.

***

So how do I handle the work/life balance now?

Simple.

I get CLEAR about what I want for that day in each area of CORE 4.

- **POWER**: I'm going to train at 7 am so I'll be up at 6, play with the dogs for a few minutes, have some coffee, leave the house at 6:30, be to the gym with my trainer at 7.

- **PASSION**: I'm going to leave a note by the coffee pot. I'm going to send a naked picture (Yes. Really.) and text to her at 11 (I set the alarm on my phone to remember). Then we have date night (which means I have already called the sitter and made the dinner reservation) at 7 pm.

- **PURPOSE**: I'll read *As A Man Thinketh*, by James Allen, and, *Crush It*, by Gary Vaynerchuk, as soon as I get home from the gym. Then, I'll do a Facebook live on my way to the office, sharing what I learned in my morning study.

- **PRODUCTION**: I'm going to make 15 sales calls before lunch. Take lunch from 12-1 and listen to *Wired for Love* on my phone. I'm going to send out one email to all prospective clients immediately after lunch and create two new marketing ads from 2-4. I meditate from 4-4:30, then do coaching calls from 4:30-6:30. After my last call wraps up, I leave office and head home for date night.

***

Here is what I've learned by utilizing CORE 4.

Every single day, 7 days a week, I have a plan.

I have specific actions set and structured in each area of CORE 4.

Every morning I wake up with a specific plan on how and when I will work out. What exactly I will do to invest in my relationships. What I will study. And an exact plan to get paid.

No ambiguity. Nothing left to chance. No CHAOS.

Just Specific and deliberate ACTION, every single day.

CORE 4 is your MAP.

Follow it, and you will get to the destination 100% of the time.

Get lost in the middle of your day? Just pick up the map you created for CORE 4 and keep going. No more bad days leading to bad weeks and bad months.

Now when I have a shitty situation come up, I deal with it then I pick up my map and keep moving forward.

The beauty of the MAP is when all the daily bullshit that comes up does indeed come up, you simply look at the map to get back on track.

When some asshole tries to derail you, you have the MAP right in front of you. You simply get back on track and follow the map.

There are no excuses with CORE 4.

CORE 4 is like the closing scene of the Matrix when Neo finally gets it. It's the moment he finally understands who and what he is. If you don't know what I'm talking about, watch the movie.

CORE 4 allows me to dodge the bullets and punches being thrown at me just like Neo did.

It does NOT mean punches are not being thrown, or shit storms quit raging, what it means is I have trained myself and built a life and system that when the punches are thrown I see them coming and I dodge them.

When the shit storm rolls in, I have already mapped a course to avoid it.

***

The beauty of having a system, the beauty of having CORE 4 is having a proven method, a proven system that trumps your emotions or feelings.

You can be having a shitty day, but if you do CORE 4, you will get a result.

Tired and don't want to get up?

Doesn't matter, I must work out and hit my CORE 4.

Mad at the wife?

Doesn't matter, I'm sending the text to hit my CORE 4.

See, we humans are programmed to take the easy path. The path of least resistance. So, when we face a challenge, or we are tasked with something difficult to do, we will make an excuse. We will get punched in the face then blame everyone and everything around us.

Making that excuse is just as easy as CHOOSING to do the work and create a result. The choice itself is equal. The power and energy are the same if you say, "fuck it I'm not doing it," as opposed to, "fuck it let's do this."

CHOOSING big is just as easy as CHOOSING small.

You cannot avoid the punches being thrown, but what you can do is learn how to avoid being punched.

This is why CHOOSING CORE 4 every day sets you up to win. It's how you avoid being punched!

Everyone reading this has the same 24 hours in a day and has the same ability to voice simple and clear words of YES or NO.

Yes, I will do it.

No, I will not do it.

"Sean, you don't get it, man. I'm busy. I'm hustling, and I can't just shut my phone off for hours at a time each night."

Sure, you can. You just don't know how and haven't made it a priority.

CORE 4 solves this problem.

***

"Sean, you don't get it, man. I run the business. If my people can't reach me, then we're in big trouble."

Bullshit.

You simply have not set up your business and home life the right way.

"Sean, you don't get it, man! My parents are fat, and I'm fat because of my genetics."

Bullshit.

You are lazy and uncommitted to getting into shape.

"Sean, you don't get it, she is a bitch and treats me like crap!"

Bullshit.

You have not taken her on CONSISTENT date nights, rubbed her feet, or told her the TRUTH in years.

***

CORE 4 solves every single problem you could ever face!

Yes, that is a bold statement, but I can prove it.

CORE 4 is the source of everything we do. It's the tool that keeps us on track. It keeps us moving forward, healthy, making more money, having more sex, connecting with friends and family, and giving our business all it needs to THRIVE.

CORE 4 is the ticket to having everything you want.

"Core 4 is a choice. It's easy to do, and it's easy not to do. When I made a choice to apply it in my life daily, it evolved me into the new me. The better me. I was lost, but now I am found! Applying core 4 in my life daily has been the difference maker in all aspects of my life!"

– David Dawson

POWER
The Body

$$* * *$$

"Being fat and unhealthy is a choice. You are not big boned. You are lazy, undisciplined, and you don't have a plan."

- Sean Whalen

$$* * *$$

Fitness is not a luxury; it is a necessity. A gym membership is not a luxury, having one is as important as having heat and lights in your home.

Your body runs it all.

It's what hugs and loves the kids; it's what punches the keyboard at work, it's what shows up at the kid's soccer games. Your body is needed to sell the clients. It's what makes love to your woman.

It doesn't matter if you go to the local park and do a circuit on the playground, or if you go to the CrossFit box and sling around weights.

Every single day of the week, you must choose to invest in your body by strengthening it through diet and fitness.

***

The first area of CORE 4 is POWER (the body)

Every single day you have a plan and purpose to sweat.

No exceptions.

Not when you feel like it.

Not when the weather is nice.

Not when it's simple and easy.

Every fucking day you work out.

Every day you make a conscious choice about what food you put in your body.

One thing I found a few years back, when I got committed to my fitness was this: The better I treated my body and the better shape I got it, the clearer my mind was. The clearer my mind was, the better my business did, the more present I was with my kids, and the better I felt all the way around.

***

Your diet and fitness are DIRECTLY connected to your business and income.

Want to make more money? GET IN BETTER SHAPE!

It does not matter how much money you have or how smart you think you are. Being overweight, eating shit all day long, is just stupid.

Would you put regular gas in a Ferrari? Nope, you'd use premium. Stop treating your body like a Ford Tempo.

I appreciate all the degrees you have hanging on the wall, but if you are not taking care of your body, you are a fucking idiot. Sure, you're working for the dollars and the freedom, but you are literally killing yourself in the process!

***

Want to have more SEX?

GET IN BETTER SHAPE!

I hear people say all the time, "I'm attracted to what's on the inside." 95% of the time it's an overweight out of shape person saying that, but let's be candid.

When you LOOK GOOD, you FEEL GOOD!

When you look good and want to take your shirt off or strut around in your panties, your sex life will be on fire. If, however, you feel fat (because you are) and you wear baggy sweats, not because they are comfortable, but because they hide what you are embarrassed by, I can guarantee you are not having as much or as good of sex as you could!

***

I once interviewed a guy for THE LIONS NOT SHEEP EXPERIENCE (lionsnotsheepexperience.com). As I was interviewing him, he told me he was significantly overweight. Over 150 lbs. overweight.

He said how he always lacked energy, and when he came home at night all he wanted to do was sit on the couch.

I like the couch as much as the next guy, but guess what? This fucking guy had four little kids!

Was he running around with them in the yard? NOPE.

Was he coaching any of their teams? NOPE.

He told me he felt so shitty because he ate like shit and did not work out that he could not ride a god damn bike down the street with his children!

Look, you are NOT big boned. You eat like hell; you don't exercise daily, so you are FAT!

I cannot think of one BENEFIT IN LIFE that comes from being obese. Not one.

So, the first order of business with CORE 4 is your diet and fitness. DAILY.

To keep it simple here is how you can IMMEDIATELY start crushing your fitness.

**

Step 1: Hire a trainer or find a workout partner.

Immediately.

Not tomorrow, or when you get a bonus check. I mean the second you close this book.

Don't know where or how to find a trainer? Do a Facebook post and ask who your friend's train with. Ask if you have any friends that are personal trainers. Go to your gym and ask if they can recommend a trainer.

It's not hard, you just have to fucking ask, and I guarantee you will find a trainer and or partner.

Having a trainer and workout partner is about accountability. It's about SIMPLICITY!

If you showed up at the office every day and had someone just telling you what to do, but you made millions in the process, that would be sweet! Everyone would do it because all you had to do was show up and do what you were told.

That is exactly why you hire a trainer. For SIMPLICITY. You don't need to think about workouts and diet, you just show up and do what you're told.

Step 2: Have a plan

If a trainer is not in your cards for whatever reason, going to the gym with no plan is pointless. You might as well just slam your head through some sheetrock and call it a day. You know damn well what I'm talking about when I say to have a plan. You do a few curls, sit on the ab machine, then walk on the treadmill for 10 minutes and call it good.

If you want ease and simplicity, hire a trainer.

I go to the gym at the same time every morning and just do what my trainer tells me. He's a professional bodybuilder and has been his whole damn life; he knows what the hell he is doing.

I don't have to worry about what I'm doing, how I'm going to do it, what order I'm going to do it in, etc., I just show up and get my ass kicked.

If you can't hire a trainer, start with a work out partner. Find a friend who wants to meet you the same time every day to get a workout in.

But, consider this as you think about a gym partner: Find someone already in shape.

Ask your friend who is in shape when they workout and if you could workout with them.

Do what they do.

Eat what they eat.

Follow their lead.

This will push you! If you go with your fat lazy friend, guess what you'll both do together at the gym? Be fat and lazy.

Either way, from the second you walk in the gym tomorrow, you better have a plan.

**

There are groups like the one I run online that are fantastic resources for fitness.

I have a mastermind group, THE LION'S DEN, made up of hundreds of people from around the globe and they live CORE 4.

We have nutritionists, gym owners, trainers, etc. in the group. Hundreds of members have reached out to these trainers and started working with them on their diet and fitness.

The other plus of THE LION'S DEN (lionsnotsheepden.com) is the opportunity to have hundreds of accountability partners. You can post your before and after photos in the group and know that dozens of others are doing the same, and getting uncomfortable, just like you.

**

Whatever you choose, you MUST IMMEDIATELY make your BODY a daily priority.

Rain or shine.

Sore or not.

EVERY SINGLE DAY.

If you must get up early in the morning to make it happen, go to bed earlier.

If you don't live near a gym, get online and figure out how to create one at home.

Learn and study diet plans, eating healthy, and fitness plans (Google is free).

There are COUNTLESS resources available to help you get this ball rolling.

However, the #1 thing you MUST be committed to every single day is this:

DOING THE FUCKING WORK!

There is NO EXCUSE for not working out and having a body that can do whatever you tell it to do.

DO THIS NOW

POWER

- **Hire a trainer.**
- Post on social media asking your friends who a good trainer is. Look some up, call a few. Find one and COMMIT to training. Saying, "I'll get back to you," or, "let's try it out," is not a commitment, paying money is a commitment.
- Pay money, set the time, and show the hell up. Even if it's a 30-day paid trial, HIRE THEM TODAY! Nothing says, "I'll be there," more than paying for the time.

- **Find and commit to an accountability partner.**
- If you cannot afford a trainer, commit TODAY to workout with someone.
- Set the time, set the location or gym, but have a plan for tomorrow to start!

- **Get rid of all your shitty food.**
- Put this book down and go throw all your garbage food out. Candy, sugars, etc. Eating healthy is NOT expensive, but being fat and sick is!
- Google 'HOW TO EAT HEALTHY' and follow some type of eating plan! Anything is better than eating shitty processed foods! I'm not going to try to sell you on this or that diet or fad; I'm simply going to say GET RID OF YOUR SHIT!
- Ask your fit friends for help. Find and ask a nutritionist! It's your choice if you put unhealthy food in your mouth, so use that same energy to figure out what is good for you!
- 75% of fitness is eating right, so get rid of the shit and start NOW!

- **Commit right now to having a plan for tomorrow.**
- Put this book down and write down exactly where you will work out tomorrow when you will work out tomorrow, and exactly what exercises you will do! Then do it the next day, and the day after that, etc.

"I have always struggled balancing my home life – relationships with my wife and kids –with running a business. The Core 4 principles that I have learned are simple yet life-changing. I am much more 'present' in all I do now, and it's paid off for myself and all those I care for and work with. Powerful teachings on how to live and how to BE!"

- Earl Koskie

PASSION

Relationships

✳✳✳

"So then, the relationship of self to other is the complete realization that loving yourself is impossible without loving everything defined as other than yourself."
- Alan Watts

✳✳✳

There is nothing that will distract you, annoy you, frustrate you, demoralize you, or cause you to go broke more quickly than shitty relationships.

I'm not just talking about with a spouse or lover. I'm talking about having drama, beef, resentment, frustration, or unresolved issues with ANY human being in your life.

Mom. Dad. Brother. Sister. Co-worker. Ex-wife, or Ex-husband, etc. Fucking EVERYONE!

You need to eliminate that shit NOW! You must look at that drama or issue like you would look at a disease.

It will eat you alive.

It will occupy and control your mind, and if you allow it, it will eventually kill you.

But here's the kicker. The disease is in YOUR body. And the only person that can remedy, cure, and rid your body of the disease, is YOU!

***

Have you ever had a bad break up, and all you want to do is lay around and eat like shit? (don't lie, fellas, you do it too but probably with alcohol.)

Relationships have a direct and serious impact on your fitness and health.

Ever had a breakup or dealt with serious family bullshit and you don't want to go to work?

Your success and income are DIRECTLY connected to your relationships.

A bad relationship will ruin your business.

A bad relationship will cause you to get fat.

A bad relationship will cloud your mind to the point that everything in your life turns to shit.

***

Imagine that your mind and soul are this perfectly round pizza. The entire pizza and all the slices represent your LOVE, PEACE, PRODUCTIVITY, and DRIVE. The pizza is essentially everything you want in life that is good. It's a clear and focused mind.

100%

But now one of the pieces of pizza is bad.

It's drama.

It's unresolved shit with someone in your life.

You think about it often.

You don't want to see them and rarely talk to them.

You had a fight before work.

Your significant other is driving you nuts for whatever reason, and you think about it all day.

This drama and this bullshit take a percent of your daily capacity—let's say 30%—is no longer dedicated to all that is good in your mind. So, now you only have 70% of all that possible power, clarity, peace and good.

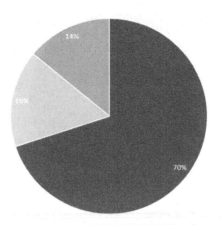

Imagine every morning leaving for the office pissed off or carrying around resentment at your lover.

You have just taken another 20% out of the pie.

Beef at work with some asshole co-worker? Another slice of the pie.

Before you know it, you have taken 60% of your mind, soul, and life, and given it away to drama, resentment, lies, bullshit, ego, pride, and any other stupid ass thing that does not make you money or make you happy.

***

How much money does drama at home make you?

Better yet, how much is the drama at home COSTING you?

I have interviewed hundreds of men from around the globe for my LIONS NOT SHEEP programs, and this one question gets them every time.

"How much money is relationship stress COSTING you?"

Most of the time they say nothing.

But, when we look deeper and consider that they are only operating at 50% capacity (remember the pizza slices), they quickly realize that drama in relationships could be costing them hundreds of thousands, or even millions of dollars a year.

***

Perhaps you have a lot of people in your life that you have issues with.

Maybe Mom or Dad did some stupid shit when you were a kid.

Maybe a boss or friend screwed you for lots of money.

Maybe your ex broke your heart or threw your life into a tailspin.

I get it; it happens to all of us.

But, at the end of it all, the drama you carry from those relationships is your fault, and you are single-handedly giving away all that power, energy, and goodness.

Yes, you read that right. IT IS YOUR FAULT.

Right now, I'm sure many of you are thinking, "but so-and-so did this or that to me, so how is that MY fault?!"

My ex was a bitch, Sean; you have no idea about my story!

I was abused as a kid, mom and dad were junkies, my brother stole my girl, etc.

Understand this one thing CLEARLY. If there is ANY DRAMA, RESENTMENT, BITTERNESS or ANGER in your life, it is 100% YOUR FAULT.

Don't agree?

Put this in your pipe and smoke it.

Road rage.

Let's say some shitty driver cuts you off. You honk at them and give them the bird, or yell something at them through the window. You honking, flipping the bird, and yelling FUCK YOU was 100% your choice.

"Yea but they cut me off!"

Yes, they did, but that driver did NOT make you react the way you did. YOU CHOSE THAT.

Now, let's take it one step further. Both you and the car that cut you off pull over. You jump out to kick his ass, and you get into a fight.

Guess what?

That physical confrontation is 100% YOUR FAULT!

NO ONE MADE YOU PULL OVER, GET OUT OF YOUR CAR AND THROW A PUNCH; YOU CHOSE THAT! 100% your choice! No matter how shitty a driver they are, no matter what they said to you, no matter how many names they called you, no matter how MAD you are or what that asshole did.

IT IS 100% YOUR FAULT FOR GETTING OUT OF THE CAR.

That was a CHOICE.

Just like being mad at someone is a CHOICE.

Just like harboring resentment is a CHOICE.

***

It is the same with your relationships.

EVERY relationship.

You and you alone are making the conscious choice to stay mad, EVEN THOUGH so and so said such and such.

Just like you made the CHOICE to get out of the car and fight, by carrying around the drama YOU and YOU ALONE are making the CHOICE to stay mad. It's the same thing.

You are giving away pieces of the pie (your mind) every single time you allow unresolved shit or other emotional BS with relationships to remain in your space.

Unresolved issues clutter your mind and steal your energy. Energy and clarity you should be using to focus on growth, not drama.

***

When I was growing up, my father was emotionally abusive to my brother and me.

When he and my mother separated, he locked us out of the house, and I only got to take a trash bag of clothes from my room and my entire childhood.

I was ANGRY at him for so many years, but then, it hit me. He didn't know any better. His dad beat the shit out of him when he was a kid, so as a father he did not know any better.

He did the best with what he had and what he knew.

Years ago, I had this realization.

Being mad at my father does not help me. It does not create anything good with him. It does not make me more money or help me build my business. It does not make me a better father or help me have six-pack abs.

So why be angry at him if it costs me?

What GOOD is being angry at him doing for me?

What POSITIVE is happening in my life by me calling him an asshole and hanging on to all the dumb shit he did.

Not a goddamn thing.

NOTHING.

Not one thing and the anger and bullshit I was hanging on to was only affecting ME!

This is why I do CORE 4 every single day! I started to see just how NEGATIVE it was for me to hang on to any of the drama or anger with him.

Once I saw that all that space in my head consumed with it cost me money, and energy, I sorted that shit out QUICKLY!

I started reaching out to him.

Messaging, texting, calling and leaving messages, sending emails.

Every single time I did I FELT BETTER!

To this day, I email my dad pictures, videos, and messages. He has not responded to me in years. He's an angry, bitter fella. But I love him, and I came to find that love not only because he's my dad, but because as I reached out, I thought less and less about all the bullshit.

So, I continue to send him pics and videos of the grandkids he's never met because every time I do, I know he sees them, and every time I hit send I FEEL GOOD!

The anger has gone away.

I made the pizza whole and regained 100% of the power through my actions alone!

"But Sean, that's you. Not me. My situation is different."

Bullshit. That's just an excuse, and you know it.

***

So how do you start to take back those pieces of the pie?

How do you start to regain the power you've lost by having so much drama?

It's simple, really.

YOU ELIMINATE EVERY ASPECT OF DRAMA IN YOUR LIFE.

You literally do the exact opposite of what you think will bring you happiness.

Instead of saying fuck you, you say I appreciate you.

Instead of ignoring the person, you reach out to the person.

This also includes eliminating specific people if need be.

Listen, you are in control of who you talk to, who you work with, who you sleep with, who you drink beer with.

You are 100% in control of the other humans you allow in your space every day.

If there is contention or unresolved issues, it's on YOU to either fix them or sever the relationship.

It's your choice to jump out of the car and hit the shitty driver, and it's your choice to stay mad at someone, no matter how big an asshole he or she may be!

***

"Yeah but Sean, I can't change the assholes at my job."

Correct. You cannot. But, you can change jobs and work with people you like. And if changing jobs isn't an option, you are still 100% in control of how you react to your co-workers. You CHOOSE every day how you're going to interact with them, and whether or not you're going to allow them to take up space in your head.

"Yea but Sean, you don't realize how big of a bitch my wife is."

Bro, if you're saying that, chances are you are as big of a dick as she is a bitch. So, first thing first, stop being a dick.

You have no control over other people. But you DO have control over yourself.

Your behavior, your reactions, your words, and your actions.

Focus on what YOU can change, stop focusing on how others act or treat you.

Creating change in relationships is the single most important, and difficult thing humans do every day. But it NEEDS to be done if YOU want to have peace, clarity, and success in your life!

So how can you create change in your relationships? You must do the most challenging thing you have ever done.

Be vulnerable.

***

One of the most powerful books I have ever read is *Dark Side of the Light Chasers*, by Debbie Ford.

In her book, she talks about vulnerability. Most people think of vulnerability (doing things that scare you, saying things that are uncomfortable, etc.) as something that is extremely difficult, and even dangerous.

Vulnerability is seen as weakness.

Saying I'm sorry means you lose.

Saying hello after years of not speaking means they've won.

BULLSHIT.

Vulnerability is the single greatest power you and I have.

I WILL SAY THIS AGAIN! VULNERABILITY IS A DAMN SUPERPOWER!

Think about the person who is terrified of public speaking and must be vulnerable on stage and give a talk. What do they say 99% of the time after they get off that stage?

"HOLY SHIT, I DID IT!"

There is a rush of adrenaline and endorphins! They are unstoppable! They feel like they could do anything!

THAT IS THE POWER OF BEING VULNERABLE!

That is the feeling we want every day. But, when you're walking around with pieces of the pie being given to other people by being angry, resentful, etc., YOU LOSE EVERY TIME!

***

Just like with POWER, PASSION requires us to make DAILY investments in our relationships.

If there is a single person in your life you feel anger, resentment, or anything negative towards, you need to reach out.

Send a text and say THANK YOU, or I APPRECIATE YOU.

Sure, you may want that person to get hit by a bus or choke on their breakfast, but you are not doing this for them.

YOU ARE DOING THIS FOR YOU!

The name of the game with PASSION is to have strong, healthy relationships with the people in your life, not half-ass, dramatic, and resentful ones.

If there is a significant other in your life, you invest in that relationship EVERY DAY through words and deeds.

Send a text message.

Leave a note.

Every single day you take a specific action, that action has a specific purpose, and is an intentional investment in that relationship.

***

One of the most valuable lessons I have learned about building good relationships is this:

THE TIME YOU DO NOT WANT TO SAY OR DO SOMETHING NICE IS THE EXACT TIME YOU MUST DO IT!

Having a great relationship with a lover is liberating.

Squashing all drama and beef with family, friends, coworkers, etc. is powerful.

So, if you want more power (at work, at the gym, with your family, etc.) eliminate every bit of anger, frustration, and resentment from your mind and life.

***

You are NOT an island, and you are NOT the only one dealing with relationship issues (at home or outside of the home).

Hundreds of members of my mastermind group, THE LION'S DEN, share their stories daily. Stories of divorce, breakup, family issues, abuse, problems with employees and co-workers, the list goes on and on.

The beauty of being around a group of people who are all willing to share their truth is that there are literally hundreds of people, right at your fingertips, who are ready and willing to help you with creating solutions!

No relationship is too far gone to invest in. Why? BECAUSE YOU ARE NOT TOO FAR GONE!

As long as there is breath in your lungs, you can be adding value to loved ones, showing appreciation, and creating exactly what you want in your life and relationships!

But, the #1 reason you must invest DAILY in your relationships is for the POWER and STRENGTH you receive by playing and operating each day with every slice of the pie intact.

YOU MUST INVEST.

You must date your lover.

You must spend time with your kids.

You must clear any and all drama from your space.

There is INFINITE power available to you when you have strong relationships around you.

CHOOSE TO CREATE THEM by investing in them DAILY!

DO THIS NOW

PASSION

-   **Send a text.**
-   Put this book down and send your wife, husband, girlfriend or boyfriend a text message telling them you appreciate them. DO NOT FUCKING THINK ABOUT IT! SEND THE TEXT NOW!
-   Set an alarm in your phone (guys this is for you because if you're like me, you need to be reminded) to do the same thing tomorrow.
-   ACTION NOW will beat your "goals" and bullshit in the future.

-   **Squash the beef.**
-   Right now, think about anyone and everyone you have drama with. Those names that just popped into your mind send them a text message. It does not matter how crazy or how deep the wounds are, SEND THEM A MESSAGE NOW! You cannot go another day carrying around that bullshit, send them the message. This will be the most

important thing you do with this book. Literally doing this shit IMMEDIATELY. Not next week or when you "feel like it," NOW.

- **Show APPRECIATION.**
- If you are married, have a significant other, or are in love and trying to build a relationship, buy a pack of sticky notes. You know, the little square sticky notes you can get at pretty much any store. Sit down with the entire pack and write a note on each one. I LOVE YOU. I LOVE YOUR BODY. I WANT TO FUCK YOU. I LOVE HOW YOU SMELL. YOU ARE BEAUTIFUL. YOU ARE MY DREAM. Etc. Draw little pictures, write inappropriate things, talk dirty. Call him or her their pet name, just use the entire pad of notes. Then take them all over your house, car, closet, underwear drawer, refrigerator, garage, tool box, etc. and stick them and stash them. This is the gift that keeps on giving! Fellas, imagine all the shoes your woman has, and imagine if she finds notes from you a month from now as she wears a pair and the note you wrote today is found. This is a such a simple way to show your appreciation and affection, and the cost is a buck or two for the notes. I've done this and had notes found months and months later!

- **Set up date night NOW.**
- If you are married and have not had consistent WEEKLY dates with your lover, START NOW!
- Fellas, DO NOT ASK HER "what do you want to do?" PLAN THAT SHIT! Find the sitter, book the night and tell your queen, "be ready at 5 pm Wednesday night and dress casual." When she asks what you are doing, tell her not to worry about it but you love her and to be ready!
- Date night is NON-NEGOTIABLE fellas (and ladies). Make it happen, mix it up, and use that time to connect. It doesn't matter if you go to a fancy dinner or take a picnic

basket of PB&J sandwiches to the park, it's being together, with no distractions and connecting.
-   NO CELL PHONES ON DATE NIGHT!

-   **Use your phone.**
-   Fellas use your phone to remind you to do things! Put alarms and reminders in your phone right now, set them up to repeat. Things like: TEXT HER AND SAY I LOVE YOU, SCHEDULE DATE NIGHT, BUY HER FLOWERS, etc. Put in your phone BUY HER FLOWERS, then have it repeat monthly. Taking 60 seconds to put this in your phone—and then actually BUYING THE FLOWERS—changes the game with her in a major way.
-   Ladies, DO THE SAME THING! Set a reminder to send him naughty pictures, to do XYZ sexual thing with him, to surprise him at his office. Use this technology to remind you to fucking invest! The beauty of doing it this way is that it'll remind you, even on the days you don't want to be nice or aren't feeling particularly sexy. THOSE ARE THE DAYS YOU NEED IT THE MOST and taking a few minutes RIGHT NOW to put that shit in your phone will pay dividends for months and months to come!

Tell the truth and be vulnerable. 24/7. 365. I do not need to explain this. Tell the truth now, tonight, tomorrow and every second of every day NO MATTER WHAT.

"Core 4 helped me save my marriage and business after my wife and I suffered the loss of a child. There is no telling where we would be without it."

- Andrew Barron

PURPOSE
The Mind & Spirit

***

"Before a man can achieve anything, even in worldly things, he must lift his thoughts above slavish animal indulgence."
- James Allen

***

Every single thing starts in the mind.

Sex
Fitness
Business
Love
Desire
Emotion
Parenting
Fighting
Fear

Everything that happens in our day-to-day world stems from our mind. From the choices we make to the things we feel.

***

My favorite book, *As A Man Thinketh,* by James Allen, is a brilliant book. I've given away hundreds of copies, that's how much I love this book. The title is a perfect description of what the book is about.

Literally, "As you think, so you are."

I heard that shit and read all the feel-good quotes for years. But when I read this book, many years ago, I started to see how it all worked.

I finally started to understand that my mind was indeed a garden and no matter what, it would bring forth and grow things.

What is grows, however, is 100% up to me.

***

What do I mean? It's simple, really.

I can do nothing with my mind (never study, never learn, never increase my skill set) and it will bring forth weeds. If I fail to manage the garden (my mind) the weeds simply take over, and undesirable things will indeed grow. Drama. Fear. Doubt. Hesitation. Lies. Resentment. Failure.

However, I can also plant good seeds and harvest good fruit by watering, nourishing, and tilling the ground of my mind.

I can inject positivity, knowledge, and tools that allow me to create a garden that not only brings forth beautiful flowers but provides me fruit that keeps me filled day after day.

This might sound hocus pocus to some of you.

Hippie bullshit, right?

But, in all honesty, nothing has helped me more than learning to control my mind.

If I cannot control and discipline my mind, I'll never create a consistent workout routine.

If I cannot control and discipline my mind, my business will never be consistent, and my income will fluctuate.

If I cannot control and discipline my mind, my anger and fear will show up over and over in my relationships.

THE MIND IS THE SOURCE OF ALL!

Movement of the body, kissing your lover, playing with the kids, building a business. ALL of this starts in the 6 inches between your ears.

***

The #1 thing we can do to plant good seeds in our mind is to inject positivity every morning. Not after the shit storm starts, or you get to the CHAOS at work, IMMEDIATELY when you roll out of bed.

Every single morning starts like this for me:

-       Wake up at 5:30.
-       Walk out to my back deck and say a little prayer thanking God for another day.
-       Walk to the bathroom and pee.

-       Then I take the dogs outside. As I'm walking down the stairs into the backyard, I'll go to YouTube and listen to Joe Rogan's video "Be the Hero of Your Own Movie."
-       Then, I'll get dressed, all the while I'm listening to motivational, positive videos.
-       I do this every morning before I leave for the gym. On the way to the gym, I listen to an audiobook in the car.

EVERY MORNING STARTS LIKE THIS!

Some of you think this is lame as shit and useless. I'm telling you, as the Almighty is my witness, WHAT YOU PUT IN YOUR BRAIN WILL GROW!

You could have had the worst night or be preparing for a huge day ahead of you at the office. The time you invest in the morning to plant positive vibes, positive words and energy in your mind will pay dividends throughout the day.

Any negative thoughts from the day before are replaced with good words, powerful music, and inspirational information.

***

Here is why this is one of my #1 morning routines:

THERE IS NO SPACE FOR BULLSHIT!

I am controlling my mind, and what goes into it from the second I wake up. Some of these videos, like the Joe Rogan one, I've listened to hundreds of times. I damn near have it memorized.

I am INTENTIONALLY putting GOOD WORDS, GOOD VIBES and GOOD THOUGHTS INTO MY MIND!

This single daily action could change your life. Do it for 90 days and see what happens.

Your days will be better.

Your workouts will be stronger.

Your connection and interactions with family and co-workers throughout the day will shift.

Your mind is the greatest supercomputer ever built. I can take my Mac and delete everything from it. I can wipe it completely clean. I can also fill it to capacity.

Our minds NEVER forget and can NEVER be filled! Our minds are STARVING for nutrients and food! So, feed it!

***

One of my all-time favorite quotes is, "Idle time is the devil's workshop."

Idle time can ruin us. Not because we are sitting around, but because our mind starts to wander and get lost. The mind needs to be tested, stretched, and fed CONSTANTLY! And just like your body, if you feed it shit it will perform like shit. If you put good messages inside it, if you feed it lessons and positivity, it will perform well.

When your mind performs well, everything else will follow.

DO THIS NOW

PURPOSE

- **Schedule your morning routine NOW!**
    - What will you read tomorrow?
    - What videos will you watch?
    - What audiobooks will you listen to on the way to work?
    - What time will you meditate?
- Have your morning planned out THE NIGHT BEFORE!

- **Study daily.**
- Every day (every morning) you should be injecting info into your brain.
- Set an alarm in the morning to read/listen/study. As mentioned earlier, your mind is a garden. If you want good shit to grow in your garden, YOU MUST PLANT GOOD SEEDS! Do nothing with the garden and weeds grow.
- You must become ruthlessly committed to daily study, so when you put this book down, plan what you will read tomorrow, and what time you will be listening to videos, etc.

- **Read these five books.**
- *As a Man Thinketh*, by James Allen
- *The Way of the Superior Man*, by David Deida
- *The Alchemist*, by Paulo Coelho
- *The Dark Side of the Light Chasers*, by Debbie Ford
- *Think & Grow Rich*, by Napoleon Hill

- **Learn to meditate.**
- Meditation is NOT some hippy-dippy bull shit thing people only do at Burning Man. The most powerful people

on this planet are learning and using this skill because meditation allows you to control your mind. It allows you to get and stay focused. It allows you to slow things down when needed.

- If you have never meditated before, go to YouTube and look up "GUIDED MEDITATION." Try one of them. Then try another one. There are hundreds of ways to meditate, TRY MANY OF THEM and figure out what you like best. I really like OM meditation. I have studied with the Ishaya monks and learned ascension meditation, but OM is my favorite.

- Use free resources like YouTube to start learning how to meditate then go deeper with whatever you find works best.

- Meditate daily.

"CORE 4 is LIFE! Implementing it into my daily life has created more money, deeper connected relationships personally and professionally & a clear focused mind every day before I go out to conquer the world. The world outside can be burning down, and I get to stay grounded with this under my belt. It really has allowed me to actively practice self-love every day by keeping my word to myself"

- Christin Griffin

PRODUCTION
Business

✳✳✳

"There is no nobility in being broke." -Sean Whalen

✳✳✳

Make money every day. Get paid every single day. If you are not doing that, what exactly are you doing?

A wise man and dear friend told me something that I will never forget: "Money is freedom."

I agree with that because I've been broke and being broke is being trapped. People have tried to reason and argue this with me for years, but the simple fact is without adequate financial resources, you are extremely limited in life. It does not mean you can't be happy, but without having money, you cannot have the freedom to do as you choose.

Now, let's take it back to the beginning of this book where I mentioned something that rings true here with regards to money and business.

HOW YOU DO ONE THING IS HOW YOU DO EVERYTHING.

If you are half-assing your body, and your relationships, I'd be willing to bet you are not in a financial place of abundance. Or at least not as abundant as you could be or want to be!

So, I'm going to break this financial conversation into two parts.

PART 1: If you have money
PART 2: If you are broke

I'm splitting this up because, to be candid, the mentality of someone who has a business and is profiting financially is much different than someone living paycheck to paycheck.

***

PART 1

Almost all my private 1:1 coaching clients are making 7+ figures a year. Most of them also have multiple businesses and revenue streams.

However, even with this financial success, most of them struggle with the same things:
·   The work/life balance.
·   Being married to the business and being unable to disconnect.
·   Scaling (making more, working less)

There is nothing that will sink the ship faster than a severe work/life imbalance.

This is what that generally looks like:

You work a lot to provide a lifestyle and security for your family. But, your family never sees you, and you never see your family. Your wife grows resentful, creating more stress and pressure. The additional stress pours over into your business, and now you grow resentful of her AND your business. So, you work more because she bitches more, and at the end of the day, it's a lose-lose situation.

This hamster wheel spins and spins until one of two things happens:

1.   You or she snaps. You end up divorced, giving half or more to her while going down a rabbit hole of self-destruction.

2.   You bring in outside eyes to help you create a map. A CORE 4 map. A map to have everything you want. The thriving business AND the home life that is healthy.

So many business owners and entrepreneurs struggle to find this balance. We feel like we are shorting the business if we don't get 20 hours of "work" in a day. But, we also feel like we are shorting ourselves and our families because, while we may have all the outward trappings of success, we have friction and chaos in our mind and heart because we are not giving our family more of what they need. US.

The cool part of all this is there are people (like me) who have gone through this exact scenario and learned the hard way by burning the candle at both ends and losing not only the $20,000,000+ a year business, but also the family. I say that's "cool" for you because now you have a resource you can use and leverage to learn what they did and did not do. How they ended up in that spot. And, before you get there yourself, you can correct course and avoid sinking your ship.

This is where a COACH is key.

Hiring a coach is not lame, and it does not make you a pussy, weak or a failure. Quite the contrary, it makes you smart as fuck! Show me the top person in ANY field, and I'll show you someone that has one or multiple coaches.

Athletes have multiple coaches. (strength, conditioning, team coaches)

Singers have voice coaches.

Actors have acting coaches.

Business owners have business coaches.

Good hell, even leaders and Presidents of countries have coaches, assistants, counselors, etc. They have a small army of people helping that one leader perform.

Learning from other's mistakes makes you smart and proactive, not weak and incapable.

Learning what others are doing to crush it and copying their blueprint saves you time, money and heartache.

It can also propel you to success that much more quickly because you can skip that painful (and expensive) learning curve!

The biggest obstacle for business owners and entrepreneurs is themselves. Pride and Ego helped build the business, but it's also how the business will crumble.

If you think you can muscle your way out of everything, or just because you have CEO next to your name you can see and do everything, you are wrong.

Good leaders know what they don't know.

Good business owners know what they don't know.

They also realize that as a leader or CEO they need to perform to the best of their ability, so anyone or anything that can help them get there is not only good for them but good for the bottom line.

A clear and powerful CEO is far more profitable than one who is "HUSTLING" 20 hours a day and feels like shit because he has not been to his son's football game all season.

***

So, as a successful business owner or entrepreneur what should your #1 top order of business be?

It does not matter if you are doing $2m or $200m.

What is the one thing you can do today to MAKE SHIT HAPPEN and MAKE MORE MONEY?

Bring in a set of fresh eyes. Hire a coach. Or even two.

Some of you already know this, but after interviewing hundreds of business owners and entrepreneurs, and having over 400+ clients around the globe, I'm still blown away by how few business owners ever actually do this (or have done this).

Look, you have a skill set.

Maximize the fuck out of that skill set! Be the baddest person on the planet at whatever the hell that is, then GET OUT OF THE WAY AND LET OTHERS DO THE SAME!

You are standing in your own way.

By choosing to not bring in outside eyes, you could literally be costing yourself and your business millions of dollars.

***

<u>PART 2</u>

If you are looking for a high five or an ass pat, you are in the wrong spot.

The title of this book should have told you what the fuck was inside, and what kind of coach and person I am.

I don't give a flying fuck about your sob story, who screwed you, who is "holding you back," who won't promote you, how much you lost before, how little your town is, how saturated your market is, or how bad the coffee is at your office.

FUCK YOUR EXCUSES!

Your financial success or failure is 110% your responsibility. There is NO ONE to blame for your lack other than yourself. It's no different than POWER and your body. If you are fat, it's not the cheeseburgers fault. If you are broke, it's not your boss' fault, your cat's fault or your parent's fault.

"Sean, you're a dick. You don't know how hard it is..." FUCK YOU.

"Sean, I have a bad back and bum knee. I can't..." FUCK YOU.

I have more shit wrong with my body than you could possibly imagine. But I'm at the gym every morning.

I lost millions in bankruptcy when the market crashed, yet I'm building multiple global businesses, while also going to all the kid's games, reading and studying daily, doing service, and giving to charity, among other things.

And I'm not the only one.

Millions of people get up every day, put the excuses and bullshit to the side, and then fucking create!

Trust me, you and your ailment are not special.

Your story is not special or unique.

Your loss is not new.

HOWEVER!

I have been part of the public education system, I grew up without a father figure or mentors, so I'm going to assume (NOT something you should EVER do, but for this example it works) that you don't know jack shit about business.

I'm going to assume you have no fucking clue how to start a business, find loans or investors, market and sell a product or service, or even build a website.

I titled this book *HOW TO MAKE SH*T HAPPEN* for a reason.

CORE 4 is the source of all my power.

It's what keeps the ball moving down the field, and on days I want to burn the whole thing to the ground, it's what keeps me sane and moving forward. It's what keeps my business moving forward, and me paid.

It's quite simply the greatest lesson, principle, or tool I could share with any human being on earth.

So, let me share with you right now HOW TO MAKE SHIT HAPPEN when it comes to getting PAID and getting money in your bank account.

***

Step 1

ADD VALUE! It works 100 out of 100 times.

Add value.

What does this mean?

ADD YOU. Give the world you. Give social media your passion, tell them who you are.

YOU ARE THE VALUE. Take your knowledge and GIVE IT TO PEOPLE!

The most successful people I have ever met share pretty much everything they know. Why? Because the more they share, the more the universe gives back.

You might think your idea is super special, but I can assure you it's worth 100x more if you share it with people.

We live in a consumption society; we are always taking. The wealthiest people on this planet GIVE, GIVE and GIVE some more.

Trust me when I tell you that you and your life are not "boring."

There are stay at home soccer mommies making MILLIONS doing YouTube videos just about their daily lives.

ADD VALUE by GIVING PEOPLE YOU!

Step 2

Get CLEAR.

This will be the most difficult thing you do. Get clear on this one question:

WHAT EXACTLY DO I WANT?

Now 99% of you just thought, "I want more money." No shit you do, you are broke.

My question back to you is: HOW MUCH MONEY?

If you are not where you want to be right now financially, you will need first to determine exactly what you want before you can start to figure out how to get it.

Write that question on your bathroom mirror, write it on your hand, put it as a reminder on your phone.

Nothing will be more important than answering this one question, WHAT EXACTLY DO I WANT.

The old saying is, "if you don't know where you are going any road will take you there."

Get CLEAR on where you want to go; then you can build a map to get there.

I have asked millionaires this question, and they cannot answer.

I have asked broke people this question, and they cannot answer.

This is the single most important question YOU CAN ANSWER.

The reason I am effective as a coach is I am a MASTER at getting people to peel back the layers of their own bull shit. Why am I a master at this? Because I spent years telling all the same lies you tell.

Answer this question, I mean REALLY fucking answer this question and your life will RADICALLY change.

Step 3

GOOGLE.

I recently Googled how to build a spaceship. I'm not kidding. Guess what I found? The god damn blueprints from NASA on how to build a spaceship!

GOOGLE how to start a business, how to find a lawyer, how to sell your shit online, how to budget, how to find a loan, how to market and sell, how to create strategies, how to find partners, how to do a YouTube video, how to post on Facebook, how to make friends, how to meditate, how to get in shape, how to save your marriage, how to be better in bed, how to be a good parent, how to speak in public, how to network, how to meet _____, how to sing, how to become a good hunter, how to write a book, how to make a movie, how to become POTUS, how to have skin like a supermodel etc, etc, etc, etc.

GOOGLE IS FUCKING FREE!

GOOGLE IS FUCKING FREE!

Did I mention GOOGLE and every single bit of information you need TO BUILD A GODDAMN SPACESHIP, start a business and make money is right at your fingertips?

If you choose to watch TiVo vs. using GOOGLE to educate yourself, you should stop lying. Stop saying you want to hustle and be a provider, and just admit you want to be a lazy, broke asshole the rest of your life.

Every answer to every question is there. Every person you need to connect with and talk to is there. Social media has over 1,000,000,000 people on it. Mark Zuckerberg built a FREE platform that can help you meet ANYONE! (Thanks, Mark).

GOOGLE can literally make you a millionaire. I'm not kidding. All the knowledge and tools are out there; you just have to get the knowledge and use the damn tools.

Step 4

COPY. Learn this word, repeat it over and over and over. This word is your friend.

COPY & STEAL (and no, I don't mean plagiarize).

If a guy is making a million dollars a year, you can be a dumb ass and try to do it "better" than him, but let me save you lots of time, lots of shitty business decision and lots of embarrassment...COPY THAT GUY!

Do the shit he's doing! Learn about his marketing, sales strategies, daily habits, product development strategies, etc. Literally COPY & STEAL what is already being done!

COPY WHAT WORKS!

Nothing I have done is original.

I've flipped over 3,700 properties in my lifetime. I had my own spin on how I did it but flipping houses ain't new! I copied what others had done for years before me and added my unique twist to it (ADDED MY VALUE) and made millions.

COPY COPY COPY.

It will save you MASSIVE amounts of TIME, and thousands, if not hundreds of thousands of dollars.

So, who exactly should you copy?

The people doing what you want to be doing, and who are AT THE TOP OF THE GAME!

***

Fredrick Eklund is one of the top real estate agents in America. He does not have some cheesy ass "professional headshot" he took with the other broke agents in his office (hint hint, he does not have broke agents in his office). He decided to share his entire life on social media. Most agents post lame ass MLS ads on their social media (because that's what their brokerage tells them to do). Fredrick shares his dogs, his husband, his newly adopted kids and photos of him doing deals.

People LOVE him, and he is at the top of the game as far as real estate agents go. Why copy the broke ass in your office who says, "this is how it's done," or, "this is how we do it."

Find the people leading. Find the people making the most in their industry. Find the people using the cutting-edge technology, building the best house, or running the most effective ads.

"The way we do it."

"This is how we do it."

"This is how you should do it."

Unless the person telling you these things is at the TOP of the food chain in your industry, tell them: "thank you, but fuck off."

There are WAY too many people copying broken systems. Leaders create systems and ways to do things BETTER.

COPY THEM. COPY THE PEOPLE AT THE TOP OF THE GAME!

Step 5

Network.

When I started flipping houses, Facebook hadn't started yet. Fast forward to today, and there are hundreds of millions of potential partners, clients, mentors, coaches, leads, salespeople, marketers, copywriters, lawyers, accountants, agents, at your fingertips.

ADD VALUE TO THESE PEOPLE.

Ask how you can help them.

When you see someone ask a question, answer if you know the answer.

If you see where your skill set could help someone, offer your assistance.

I have done more deals through networking than anything else.

I know more millionaires and billionaires because of networking than anything else.

Networking does not mean adding a bunch of high school buddies on Facebook and talking shit about football.

Networking on social media means seeking out experts in industries, people you'd like to do business with, like to sell to, like to partner with, and connecting with them.

There are local investment clubs all over the country. (I'm sure all over the world!) Find them (GOOGLE) and go! Meet people, shake hands, kiss babies and make yourself known!

Say hello, comment on pictures and videos, share links to educational and beneficial articles, just introduce yourself and say hello!

Technology has taken away the face to face reality of a lot of relationships. The solution is to keep meeting face to face and use technology to meet people and become friends with them virtually!

***

In 2016 I spent 4 days in the Virgin Islands on a 100-foot yacht with my good friend Mark Evans. He chartered the yacht for himself and his family, and he invited me down for a few days.

What makes this story rad is that I met Mark and his wife face to face for the first time on that boat.

We had never met face to face before, we only communicated and connected via phone, Facetime, and social media.

Mark is a big cigar fan. So am I. He and I started connecting about who knows what on social media, then one day he sent me a selfie smoking a stogie and a note saying, "MAKE IT AN EPIC DAY!" Later that day I was smoking a stogie and sent him a selfie and said, "YOU TOO MAN!"

Over the last few years, we have sent dozens and dozens of selfies smoking stogies and some little message. This friendship began by simply being a good person and saying, "hello" online.

If you start doing these five things right now, start doing CORE 4 every single day, you will win. It's that simple.

You cannot wait until tomorrow; you must start now.

DO THIS NOW

PRODUCTION

- **Hire a coach.**
- It does not matter what you do, or what your job is, hire a coach. Every successful person has a coach/mentor. Why? Because these people know what they don't know, so they hire people to help them figure it out and know what they don't know! Sure, you can bang your head against the wall even more, but hiring a coach gets you the answers you are looking for NOW, and in most cases with a lot less stress and a lot less potential for losing money.

- **Join a mastermind.**
- Join a mastermind group of people both in your industry, and a group of people outside of your industry.

You have heard the old saying, "you are who your friends are," and that is TRUTH! So, if you want to make more money, be in a group of people who are making more money!

- You should always be leveling up and growing, and the very best way is to have people in your space, in your mastermind that are doing the same thing.
- I started the mastermind group THE LIONS DEN (lionsnotsheepden.com) to share not only CORE 4 with people but to share what works for me in my life. Everything from business, to fitness and relationships, to how I eliminate CHAOS from my life. Being in a mastermind or coaching group is like having a partner available 24/7. Any question you have, frustration in your life or problem you need a solution for you have a group of people at your fingertips to reach out to.

- **If you do not love what you do, quit doing what you are doing immediately.**
- Making money is not difficult, finding or creating a job is not difficult if you have a skill set, but nothing will cause you more stress, more struggle or more problems than hating what you do and feeling like you must do it day in and day out. There are MILLIONS of people that have done exactly this, quit doing what they don't want to be doing to do something they do. Now, most of you are saying, "yea that's easy for you to say but I have bills and responsibilities." So do I, friend. But I was asked a question years ago that changed my life forever, and the question is this: "WHY DO ANYTHING YOU DO NOT WANT TO DO?" 99.9% of people will make up a ton of bullshit excuses but ask yourself that question. Why are you doing something if you don't want to do? No one is FORCING you to be at your job. No one is FORCING you to be unhappy. You are choosing both. So, if you DO NOT

like what you do, STOP DOING IT, and start doing what you like!

-   **Google. Use it!**
-   Every answer to every question you could ask is answered through Google. Don't believe me? Ask Google a question, and it'll give you an answer. Sex. Money. Religion. Family. Kids. Etc. ANYTHING.
    -   Want to start a business? Google has the answer.
    -   Want to make more money? Google can help you.
-   Want to start a brand-new career? Google will give you millions of suggestions, tips, ideas, and lessons on how to do it.
-   All your money questions can be answered, and all your money problems can be remedied by using Google

"Before I implemented Core 4 into every part of my life, I was a lost university student, overweight, and in a relationship that was holding me back. After a year of making it a priority, I've started a new university program with a laser focused vision of how I want to make money, I'm down almost 30 pounds, and I got out of that toxic relationship."

-Joshua George

CONCLUSION

✳✳✳

CORE 4 is life.

It is not a 4, 8, 12 or 200 step process to making shit happen.

It is not a series of goals or wishes that you HOPE will come to reality someday.

It is not something you put off until you have the money or have a better job.

CORE 4 is literally a way of being.

It is a way of life.

It is a lifestyle that will cause you to be INTENTIONAL with everything you do.

CORE 4 is how you make more money!

CORE 4 is how you create better relationships!

CORE 4 is how you eliminate the drama!

CORE 4 is as important to me as drinking water or sleeping. It is as important as food.

I have practiced and exercised CORE 4 for so long that it has become 2nd nature to me.

Investing in your BODY, your RELATIONSHIPS, your MIND and your BUSINESS every single day of the year with specific intention and purpose.

Doing the simple shit every single day that gets you the results you want.

Eliminating the CHAOS through specific action.

THIS IS CORE 4.

It took me almost two years of daily practice before it became 2nd nature. I did it (or said I did it) because it was the cool thing to do at the time I was learning it. I was still stuck in some patterns of bullshit, and my results ended up showing it. Just like I said FUCK IT and followed my buddy into a coaching program, I finally got tired of shitty results, so I dove all in on CORE 4.

It radically changed my life forever.

Once you realize how EVERYTHING comes from you, you realize how much you need to invest in you! We spend all this time as humans investing in a 401k, a retirement account etc., when the single greatest investment we could ever make is in ourselves and our learning.

I have things written down every day, and I have become so accustomed to investing in myself and getting CORE 4 done every morning that it is now who I am.

It's my way of life.

I listen to videos every morning,

I read every morning.
Even when I feel like shit I go to the gym and workout.

I continue to email my father.

I invest daily with my children and loved ones.

I have specific actions every day to accomplish financial and business goals.

I have multiple coaches in my life.

I also know if shit is not going right in my life, for whatever reason, it has to do with me lacking on my CORE 4. I can identify it simply by looking at what I am NOT doing every day, or what I have failed to do.

I have hundreds of clients around the globe, and every single one of them has learned CORE 4 and they work it every day.

Business owners.

Entrepreneurs.

Single moms (and dads).

Athletes.

Employees.

Old.

Young.

Every single person is creating the same structure and daily habits to get success.

A network of people working hard and pushing each other.

Hundreds of people investing in themselves to get bigger and better results.

When one of them calls me with a concern my first question is, "How is your Core 4?" When they post in the private group and say something is not right, the first thing we look at is CORE 4. When they celebrate success, it is usually due to a win with CORE 4!

Everyone today is looking for the easy pill. The quick fix to get skinny, get laid and make mounds of cash. There may be some shit available via late night infomercial to help your manhood grow, but at the end of the day, every single result we get in life comes from one simple thing.

WORK.

CORE 4 is work. Hard work. Every day.

CORE 4 will not do itself.

CORE 4 is not some check system that automatically solves the issues, pays the bills, or fixes the marriage.

CORE 4 is literally a system that—when repeated over and over again—will create habits.

Those habits will produce powerful results.
Those powerful results are what change your life.

Daily investments and work into your relationship will produce good results.

Daily investments and work on your body will get you in shape.

Daily investments on your mind will plant seeds that will bring forth good fruit.

Daily investments in your business will create stability and financial abundance.

BUT, they must all work together.

It's not called the CORE 3 or the CORE 3 ½. It's called the CORE 4 for a reason.

A table has four legs for a reason. It's sturdy and can carry a TON of weight if all four legs are intact and strong. But, if you pull one or two of the legs out, the table falls. If one of the legs is weak, the table falls. It's that simple.

If you want a secure table that is reliable, you have to have four sturdy legs.

If you want a secure life, you must do every aspect of CORE 4 every single day.

And for the record, NO ONE is lost. NO ONE is too far gone to start. NO ONE is too fat, too broke, or too fucked up to start doing the work on CORE 4 right this very second.

Remember how we eat the elephant?

ONE BITE AT A TIME!

It's a choice.

It's a personal decision.

Do you want to change the direction of your life or not?

Do you want to get different results or not?

If the answer is YES, then do the things we discussed in this book. It's that straight forward and that simple.

DO. THE. WORK.

I can't make you do it.

A coach can't make you do it.

This book can't make you do it.

You must CHOOSE.

No matter where you came from, no matter how broke you have been, not matter how deep and dark the past is, no matter how long you have been lying, no matter how much you have cheated, no matter how disconnected your relationship is, YOU CAN CHOOSE TO DO WHATEVER THE FUCK YOU WANT RIGHT NOW!

Right here. Right now.

So, CHOOSE.

***

So many people ask me the same question.

"Sean, I'm not satisfied or really happy with where I am in my life, how can I change that?"

"Sean, I'm tired of being broke and living paycheck to paycheck."

"Sean, I'm tired of feeling like I take two steps forward then 8 backward."

"How can I change things?"

My answer to that question is the same every time.

My answer to that question is probably the best way I can wrap this book up.

The answer is not a high five or ass pat that most other coaches will give you because the truth of it is most of you will put this book down and not do jack shit with it. That's just the truth.

Many of you will make excuses about how your burden is too heavy, how your past is too difficult, how your mom didn't love you enough, and how your teacher in 3rd grade didn't include you in the class project.

Blah. Blah. Blah.

So, my answer is simply this.

DO THE FUCKING WORK.

Right here.

Right now.

Not tomorrow.

Not when you get paid.

Not when it's comfortable or convenient.

You are literally a creator of your own reality. You are powerful beyond measure. You are a KING or a QUEEN. You are NOT broken. You are NOT lost.

You are EXACTLY where you need to be.

So, put all your bullshit to the side, and GO TO WORK.

NOW.

Create the life you want.

Take a small bite. Then another. Then another.

Literally put this book down right now and DO THE FUCKING WORK.

Made in the USA
Coppell, TX
25 August 2021

61217605R00066